THE OFFIC...

Arsenal

ANNUAL 2019

Written by Josh James
Designed by Chris Dalrymple

A Grange Publication

Manufactured and distributed under licence by Grange Communications Ltd., Edinburgh. Printed in the EU.

Every effort has been made to ensure the accuracy of information within this publication but the publishers cannot be held responsible for any errors or omissions. Views expressed are those of the author and do not necessarily represent those of the publishers or the football club.

Photographs © Arsenal Football Club, PA Images and Shutterstock.

ISBN 978-1-911287-99-5

CONTENTS

It is a great honour for me to be at Arsenal, and I have big ambitions for the future of the football club.

From the first moment I came here, I have been made to feel very welcome by everyone around the club, especially the supporters, and I know how important the fans will be if we are to achieve big things together.

I always say that football clubs are like one table with four legs. All the legs are very important. One leg is the organisation, the structure of the club; the second leg is the team and the players; the third is the media who broadcast our success all around the world; and the fourth is the supporters.

The four legs are very important for the table and likewise for Arsenal. If you lose one leg, you break the table. This is how I would describe our relationship with the supporters.

So I am really excited to get to know the club better, to get to know the supporters, and for us to all work together, to keep moving the club forward, always.

Of course, I already knew a lot about the history of Arsenal, and about the great name the club has all over the world, but I have been finding out more ever since I joined.

For me, I can tell you that I promise to work hard every day on the training pitches to bring success here, and I will also make sure that our players will work and work and work, and bring a huge energy to every game we play.

I want ambition from this team, I want them to be ambitious in every match. I want them to be in every match for the whole 90 minutes and to give everything they have. I want that every day, this is my ambition.

With our fans behind us as well, we want to make this a season to remember.

Unai Emery

ROLL OF HONOUR

League champions:

1931, 1933, 1934, 1935, 1938, 1948, 1953, 1971, 1989, 1991, 1998, 2002, 2004

FA Cup winners:

1930, 1936, 1950, 1971, 1979, 1993, 1998, 2002, 2003, 2005, 2014, 2015, 2017

League Cup winners:

1987, 1993

European Fairs Cup winners:

1970

European Cup Winners' Cup winners:

1994

Charity/Community Shield winners:

1930, 1931, 1933, 1934, 1938, 1948, 1953, 1991 (shared), 1998, 1999, 2002, 2004, 2014, 2015, 2017

2017/18 SEASON IN REVIEW

AUGUST

The season started with a penalty shoot-out win over Chelsea at Wembley to earn the club's 15th Community Shield, and the seventh under Arsène Wenger. Sead Kolasinac scored on his debut to level the scores in the second half, and Olivier Giroud converted the winning spot kick in the new 'ABBA' format of shootouts. The Premier League campaign kicked off on a Friday night, and started with a bang – Arsenal edging a seven-goal thriller against Leicester City. Alexandre Lacazette scored our first league goal of the season, just two minutes into his first Emirates appearance, and Giroud grabbed a late winner. But the first two away games of the season were a different story entirely. Stoke City earned a narrow 1-0 win before Liverpool ran out convincing 4-0 victors at Anfield. The month ended with Alex Oxlade-Chamberlain joining the Reds after rejecting the offer of a new contract.

ARSENAL.COM
PLAYER OF THE MONTH:
SEAD KOLASINAC

August 2017 Results	
Sun 6 - Chelsea (N)	1-1 (Won on penalties)
Kolasinac	Community Shield
Fri 11 - Leicester City (H)	4-3
Lacazette, Welbeck, Ramsey, Giroud	Premier League
Sat 19 - Stoke City (A)	0-1
–	Premier League
Sun 27 - Liverpool (A)	0-4
–	Premier League

SEPTEMBER

Two goals from Danny Welbeck, either side of a Lacazette cracker, gave the Gunners a much-needed win over Bournemouth to start September, and the club's first-ever Europa League campaign also started with a win, at home to German side Cologne. Kick off was delayed for an hour, due to the number of away fans who had descended on Emirates Stadium, but the night finished on a high thanks to goals from Kolasinac, Alexis and Hector Bellerin. It was an unbeaten month in all competitions. A well-deserved goalless draw at Chelsea was followed by a home win over Doncaster Rovers in the Carabao Cup, and 2-0 victory against West Brom in which Lacazette claimed two more. The French striker was enjoying a productive start to his Arsenal career. Rob Holding scored his first Arsenal goal in the 4-2 win over BATE Borisov in Belarus. Arsenal were fielding a young side in the competition, but this made it six points out of six in the Europa League group stage.

ARSENAL.COM
PLAYER OF THE MONTH:
NACHO MONREAL

September 2017 Results	
Sat 9 - Bournemouth (H)	3-0
Welbeck 2, Lacazette	Premier League
Thur 14 - Cologne (H)	3-1
Kolasinac, Alexis, Bellerin	Europa League
Sun 17 - Chelsea (A)	0-0
—	Premier League
Wed 20 - Doncaster Rovers (H)	1-0
Walcott	Carabao Cup
Mon 25 - West Brom (H)	2-0
Lacazette 2	Premier League
Thur 28 - BATE Borisov (A)	4-2
Walcott 2, Holding, Giroud (pen)	Europa League

OCTOBER

Another comfortable home win, this time over Brighton, continued our good form into the new month. But another away day disappointment checked the Gunners' progress. Despite taking the lead through Per Mertesacker, Watford came back to earn a controversial 2-1 win. Arsenal bounced back with a Europa League win, this time in Belgrade, thanks to a superb late goal from Giroud. Arsenal finally recorded a first away win in the Premier League with a 5-2 demolition of Everton at Goodison Park, with five different players on target. Just two days later the Emirates faithful had a new hero to worship. In the fourth round of the Carabao Cup Arsenal were trailing Norwich City 1-0 with less than 10 minutes to go. On came 18-year-old striker Eddie Nketiah for his home debut, and just 15 seconds later he'd scored a dramatic equaliser. It got even better for the teenager in first-half extra-time when he scored an unforgettable winner, sending Arsenal into the quarter-final. The month ended with Aaron Ramsey netting his 50th goal for the club in a 2-1 win over Swansea.

ARSENAL.COM
PLAYER OF THE MONTH:

SEAD KOLASINAC

October 2017 Results	
Sun 1 - Brighton & HA (H)	2-0
Monreal, Iwobi	Premier League
Sat 14 - Watford (A)	1-2
Mertesacker	Premier League
Thur 19 - Red Star (A)	1-0
Giroud	Europa League
Sun 22 - Everton (A)	5-2
Monreal, Ozil, Lacazette, Ramsey, Alexis	Premier League
Tue 24 - Norwich City (H)	2-1
Nketiah 2	Carabao Cup
Sat 28 - Swansea City (H)	2-1
Kolasinac, Ramsey	Premier League

NOVEMBER

After an uneventful goalless draw at home to Serbian side Red Star in the Europa League, there was a setback in the Premier League with a 3-1 defeat away to Manchester City – substitute Lacazette claimed the consolation goal. But it was all smiles after the international break. Shkodran Mustafi and Alexis scored to see off Tottenham in the north London derby at Emirates Stadium. Arsène Wenger's men stayed in sixth position, but the gap was closing, and a dramatic last-minute penalty by Alexis the following Sunday at Burnley was enough for a 1-0 win. It lifted the team into the top four for the first time since the opening weekend. This victory was followed three days later by a seventh straight home league win this season. Mesut Ozil inspired the Gunners to a 5-0 thrashing of Huddersfield, scoring once and adding two assists. The team had recovered well from a surprise 1-0 defeat in Germany in the Europa League, but with 10 points from five group games, the side had already guaranteed top spot and a place in the knockout stages.

ARSENAL.COM
PLAYER OF THE MONTH:
MESUT OZIL

November 2017 Results		
Thur 2 - Red Star (H)	0-0	
–	Europa League	
Sun 5 - Man City (A)	1-3	
Lacazette	Premier League	
Sat 18 - Tottenham (H)	2-0	
Mustafi, Alexis	Premier League	
Thur 23 - Cologne (A)	0-1	
	Europa League	
Sun 26 - Burnley (A)	1-0	
Alexis (pen)	Premier League	
Wed 29 - Huddersfield (H)	5-0	
Lacazette, Giroud 2, Alexis, Ozil	Premier League	

DECEMBER

Arsenal dominated as Manchester United visited Emirates Stadium early in the month, but found United goalkeeper David de Gea in excellent form, and lost 3-1 despite raining in 33 shots on goal. It was a tough blow for the Gunners, who ultimately paid the price for individual early mistakes against United. Victory would have put Arsenal within a point of second place, but the first home defeat of the season seemed to shake the players' confidence, and it was followed by disappointing draws at Southampton and West Ham. Ozil scored a fantastic volley at home to Newcastle to get the team back to winning ways, and Welbeck kept the Carabao Cup dream alive with the only goal against West Ham in the quarter-final. The real drama came around Christmas time. After trailing 2-0 at home to Liverpool, Arsenal mounted a stirring comeback, scoring three times in five minutes to turn the match around, only to concede again and have to settle for a point from a pulsating match. There were more goals six days later in a 3-2 win at Crystal Palace, but 2017 finished amid controversy and dropped points at West Brom. It looked as though Alexis's deflected free-kick had earned a late win, but referee Mike Dean awarded a dubious penalty for handball against Calum Chambers in the last minute, and the Baggies grabbed a point. It was a frustrating end to the year, but at least the Europa League group stage had been rounded off with a 6-0 dismantling of BATE Borisov.

ARSENAL.COM
PLAYER OF THE MONTH:
MESUT OZIL

December 2017 Results		
Sat 2 - Man United (H)		**1-3**
Lacazette		Premier League
Thur 7 - BATE Borisov (H)		**6-0**
Debuchy, Walcott, Wilshere, Polyakov (og), Giroud (pen), Elneny		Europa League
Sun 10 - Southampton (A)		**1-1**
Giroud		Premier League
Wed 13 - West Ham United (A)		**0-0**
—		Premier League
Sat 16 - Newcastle United (H)		**1-0**
Ozil		Premier League
Tue 19 - West Ham United (H)		**1-0**
Welbeck		Carabao Cup
Fri 22 - Liverpool (H)		**3-3**
Alexis, Xhaka, Ozil		Premier League
Thur 28 - Crystal Palace (A)		**3-2**
Mustafi, Alexis 2		Premier League
Sun 31 - West Brom (A)		**1-1**
McClean (og)		Premier League

JANUARY

2018 began with another fast-paced, action-packed fixture at Emirates Stadium, that featured more late excitement. Jack Wilshere fired the Gunners into the lead just after the hour mark against Chelsea, only for the points to have seemingly slipped away when the visitors made it 2-1 with six minutes remaining. Bellerin proved the saviour though, striking from long range in injury time to level again. That was the first of three meetings with Chelsea in January – the teams also met over two legs in the Carabao Cup semi-final. After a goalless away draw, it was Arsenal who prevailed, thanks to an Antonio Rudiger own goal and a trademark Granit Xhaka strike. A place at Wembley was booked, but Arsenal would not be going there in the FA Cup. For the first time in Arsène Wenger's reign he suffered elimination at the third round stage, when an underperforming side were beaten 4-2 by Championship side Nottingham Forest. Once again the team paid the price for conceding penalties – for the third match in a row.

The excitement came off the pitch at the end of the month. Henrikh Mkhitaryan arrived from Manchester United in exchange for Alexis – whose contract was winding down – and prolific striker Pierre-Emerick Aubameyang became the club's record signing when he joined from Borussia Dortmund. Ozil also committed his future to the club, and a new sense of optimism surrounded Arsenal, despite the ongoing troubles in away games. Swansea was the scene of the latest defeat on the road, as the month drew to a close.

ARSENAL.COM
PLAYER OF THE MONTH:

MOHAMED ELNENY

January 2018 Results	
Wed 3 - Chelsea (H)	2-2
Wilshere, Bellerin	Premier League
Sun 7 - Nottingham Forest (A)	2-4
Mertesacker, Welbeck	FA Cup
Wed 10 - Chelsea (A)	0-0
–	Carabao Cup
Sun 14 - Bournemouth (A)	1-2
Bellerin	Premier League
Sat 20 - Crystal Palace (H)	4-1
Monreal, Iwobi, Koscielny, Lacazette	Premier League
Wed 24 - Chelsea (H)	2-1
Rudiger (og), Xhaka	Carabao Cup
Tue 30 - Swansea City (A)	1-3
Monreal	Premier League

FEBRUARY

Aubameyang wasted no time in announcing his arrival at the club, scoring a fine goal after being set up by former Dortmund teammate Mkhitaryan in a 5-1 beating of Everton. That was one of three assists for Mkhitaryan on his home debut, but Ramsey went even better by netting a hat-trick of goals in another resounding Emirates display. Aubameyang couldn't repeat the heroics at Wembley in a narrow north London derby defeat, and there was further bad news when Lacazette was ruled out for six weeks with injury picked up against Tottenham. With Aubameyang cup-tied, Arsenal resumed the Europa League campaign in the small Swedish town of Ostersunds without their two main front-men, but were too good on the snow-covered plastic pitch, winning 3-0 in the first leg, eventually going through 4-2 on aggregate after a surprising return leg defeat at Emirates. To be fair, attention had probably already switched to the Carabao Cup final against Manchester City by now, but this would prove a day to forget. Sergio Aguero put City ahead inside 20 minutes and it was always difficult from then on, with Pep Guardiola's side finally running out 3-0 winners.

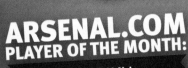

**ARSENAL.COM
PLAYER OF THE MONTH:**

HENRIKH MKHITARYAN

February 2018 Results	
Sat 3 - Everton (H)	**5-1**
Ramsey 3, Koscielny, Aubameyang	Premier League
Sat 10 - Tottenham (A)	**0-1**
—	Premier League
Thur 15 - Ostersunds (A)	**3-0**
Monreal, Papagiannopoulos (og), Ozil	Europa League
Thur 22 - Ostersunds (H)	**1-2**
Kolasinac	Europa League
Sun 25 - Manchester City (N)	**0-3**
—	Carabao Cup

MARCH

Just four days after the Carabao Cup final, runaway Premier League leaders Manchester City repeated the 3-0 scoreline at Emirates Stadium, to inflict only the second home defeat of the season, but worse followed when struggling Brighton secured a 2-1 win on the south coast – Aubameyang's goal couldn't spark a comeback. So the team were under huge pressure as they travelled to Italy for the first leg of the Europa League Round of 16 tie against AC Milan. The Serie A side were on a 13-match unbeaten run, but Arsène Wenger's men rose to the occasion, scoring twice by half-time, and taking a commanding lead back to north London. Before that second leg Arsenal hosted Watford in the Premier League. Petr Cech's first penalty save in Arsenal colours was the highlight, along with Mkhitaryan's first goal at Emirates and Aubameyang adding to his growing tally. Cech's save guaranteed his 200th career Premier League clean sheet, while the first goal of the afternoon, scored by Shkodran Mustafi, was Arsenal's 1,000th at home in Premier League history. The Europa League job was duly completed against AC Milan with a 3-1 second-leg win, in which Welbeck scored a brace. The team then had more than two weeks without a game.

ARSENAL.COM
PLAYER OF THE MONTH:
HENRIKH MKHITARYAN

March 2018 Results

Thur 1 - Manchester City (H)	0-3	Premier League
Sun 4 - Brighton & HA (A) Aubameyang	1-2	Premier League
Thur 8 - AC Milan (A) Mkhitaryan, Ramsey	2-0	Europa League
Sun 11 - Watford (H) Mustafi, Aubameyang, Mkhitaryan	3-0	Premier League
Thur 15 - AC Milan (H) Welbeck 2 (1 pen), Xhaka	3-1	Europa League

APRIL

The goals kept coming at Emirates Stadium in April. Aubameyang and the returning Lacazette scored braces in the wins over Stoke City and CSKA Moscow respectively, and then Welbeck claimed two in a 3-2 victory against Southampton. But the strike that was to be named Arsenal Goal of the Season came from Ramsey in the home leg against CSKA. Taking Ozil's cross first time, he flicked the ball over the keeper with the outside of his right foot. It was a stunning piece of imagination that set Arsenal well on the way to the final four of the competition. The Russians gave the Gunners a scare in the second leg, leading 2-0 on the night, but in-form duo Welbeck and Ramsey scored to send Arsenal through. After another domestic away day reverse – this time at St James' Park Newcastle – the club made an announcement that shocked world football. After nearly 22 years in charge, Arsène Wenger was to leave. Arsenal's longest-serving and most successful ever boss would depart at the end of the season, and the news was still sinking in as West Ham were beaten 4-1 at home. Full focus was on European football a few days later, as Atletico Madrid visited for the first leg of the Europa League semi-final. There was an incredible atmosphere inside Emirates Stadium, and Arsenal dominated against the 10-man La Liga side. Lacazette gave Arsenal a richly deserved lead, but the Spaniards struck a valuable, late away goal out of nothing. The month ended with a disappointing injury-time defeat at Old Trafford, on the day young defender Konstantinos Mavropanos made his debut.

ARSENAL.COM
GOAL OF THE SEASON:
AARON RAMSEY V CSKA MOSCOW (H)

April 2018 Results	
Sun 1 - Stoke City (H)	3-0
Aubameyang 2 (1 pen), Lacazette (pen)	Premier League
Thur 5 - CSKA Moscow (H)	4-1
Ramsey 2, Lacazette 2 (1 pen)	Europa League
Sun 8 - Southampton (H)	3-2
Aubameyang, Welbeck 2	Premier League
Thur 12 - CSKA Moscow (A)	2-2
Welbeck, Ramsey	Europa League
Sun 15 - Newcastle United (A)	1-2
Lacazette	Premier League
Sun 22 - West Ham United (H)	4-1
Monreal, Ramsey, Lacazette 2	Premier League
Thur 26 - Atletico Madrid (H)	1-1
Lacazette	Europa League
Sun 29 - Manchester United (A)	1-2
Mkhitaryan	Premier League

MAY

Try as they might, Arsenal could not find a way past the resolute Atletico Madrid defence in the second leg of the Europa League semi-final. The hosts scored at the end of the first half through Diego Costa, but the Gunners just needed one goal to take the game to extra-time. The Atletico defence stood firm, bringing an end to the European journey, and consigning Arsenal to another season without Champions League football next year.

All that remained in this campaign was to give the manager the send-off he deserved. His final home game in charge was a celebration of 22 remarkable seasons. Emirates was resplendent, with home fans decked out in 'Merci Arsène' red tee shirts, and the sun was shining as the team turned on the style on the pitch – Aubameyang scored twice in a 5-0 win over Burnley to rubber-stamp a sixth-place finish. The Gabon striker netted again in a 3-1 defeat at Leicester then claimed his 10th of the season in an emotional farewell game at Huddersfield – the 1,235th and final match of the Arsène Wenger era.

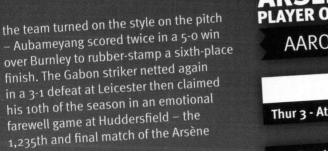

ARSENAL.COM
PLAYER OF THE SEASON:
AARON RAMSEY

May 2018 Results	
Thur 3 - Atletico Madrid (A)	0-1
—	Europa League
Sun 6 - Burnley (H)	5-0
Aubameyang 2, Lacazette, Kolasinac, Iwobi	Premier League
Wed 9 - Leicester City (A)	1-3
Aubameyang	Premier League
Sun 13 - Huddersfield (A)	1-0
Aubameyang	Premier League

MERCI ARSÈNE

Arsenal's most successful manager ever brought an end to his remarkable reign last season, bidding an emotional farewell to supporters after nearly 22 years in charge.

Arsène Wenger's time at the club began way back in October 1996 with a 2-0 win at Blackburn – 1,235 matches and 716 victories later the incredible, record-breaking tenure came to an end.

The Frenchman had changed the face of Arsenal during that time. He led the club into a new era at Emirates Stadium, reshaped the identity of the squad and oversaw the move to a new training ground. But it's his incredible achievements on the pitch that truly set him apart.

He won both the league title and FA Cup in 1997/98 (his first full season in charge) then did it again in 2001/02. They were only the seventh and eighth instances of a side winning the domestic double in the past 100 years of English football. But he wasn't finished there. After lifting another FA Cup in 2003 he created the famous 'Invincibles' side of 2004 – going down in history by winning the Premier League title undefeated. The unbeaten streak stretched into the following season – 49 games in all – an all-time record in English football.

Shortly afterwards the Gunners reached their first ever Champions League final, losing 2-1 to Barcelona, but in 2014 Wenger was celebrating silverware again – claiming his fifth FA Cup. He retained the trophy the following year, and in 2017 set a new record for seven FA Cup wins as boss with a memorable 2-1 defeat of Chelsea.

At the start of last season he beat the same opposition to win the Community Shield – his 17th and final honour with Arsenal.

His last game in charge was the 1-0 victory at Huddersfield Town on the final day of the season, a week after he said goodbye to the Emirates faithful with a 5-0 thrashing of Burnley.

Here are some of the stats and facts from the most extraordinary, most successful and most transformative reign of any manager in Arsenal history.

HONOURS

FA Cup	Community Shield	Premier League
1998	1998/99	1997/98
2002	1999/2000	2001/02
2003	2002/03	2003/04
2005	2004/05	
2014	2014/15	
2015	2015/16	
2017	2017/18	

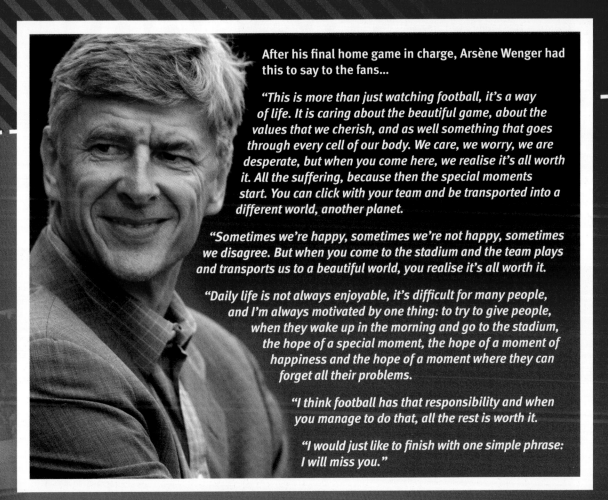

After his final home game in charge, Arsène Wenger had this to say to the fans...

"This is more than just watching football, it's a way of life. It is caring about the beautiful game, about the values that we cherish, and as well something that goes through every cell of our body. We care, we worry, we are desperate, but when you come here, we realise it's all worth it. All the suffering, because then the special moments start. You can click with your team and be transported into a different world, another planet.

"Sometimes we're happy, sometimes we're not happy, sometimes we disagree. But when you come to the stadium and the team plays and transports us to a beautiful world, you realise it's all worth it.

"Daily life is not always enjoyable, it's difficult for many people, and I'm always motivated by one thing: to try to give people, when they wake up in the morning and go to the stadium, the hope of a special moment, the hope of a moment of happiness and the hope of a moment where they can forget all their problems.

"I think football has that responsibility and when you manage to do that, all the rest is worth it.

"I would just like to finish with one simple phrase: I will miss you."

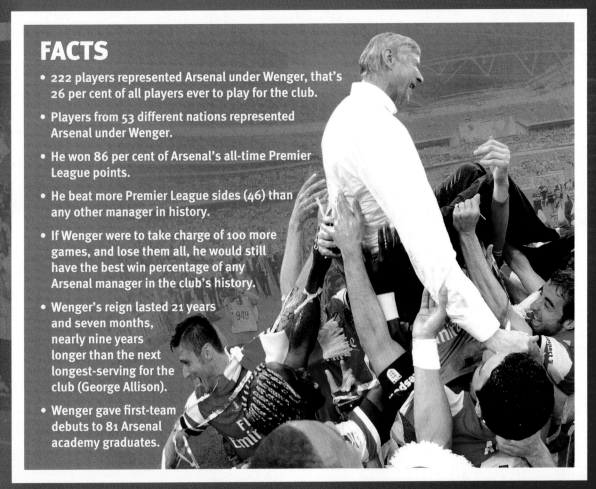

FACTS

- 222 players represented Arsenal under Wenger, that's 26 per cent of all players ever to play for the club.

- Players from 53 different nations represented Arsenal under Wenger.

- He won 86 per cent of Arsenal's all-time Premier League points.

- He beat more Premier League sides (46) than any other manager in history.

- If Wenger were to take charge of 100 more games, and lose them all, he would still have the best win percentage of any Arsenal manager in the club's history.

- Wenger's reign lasted 21 years and seven months, nearly nine years longer than the next longest-serving for the club (George Allison).

- Wenger gave first-team debuts to 81 Arsenal academy graduates.

DRESSING ROOM SECRETS

We find out what really goes on inside the Emirates Stadium dressing room...

What are you like in the dressing room before the game?

Alex Iwobi: I'm normally relaxed. I listen to music in the changing room and I'm chilled out. I like to relax my mind before the game.

Petr Cech: I speak to people when I come back from the warm up. Usually just individually, when I want something from them or to remind them of something. For example, set play organisation from corners or walls on free-kicks. So generally I'll just walk around and tell people what I'm thinking, what would help me in the game and what I would want them to do while defending. Little things like that are things that I do, but it's purely match-related.

Nacho Monreal: I have a lot of rituals. Before going out to warm up I always pray. Then when we go out onto the pitch, I jump and then my first step is always with my right foot, even though I'm left-footed. It's superstition because I changed it for a few games a few years ago, and I didn't play well. I started doing it again and played well again, so I think I'll do it until I retire.

Rob Holding: I have my music on when I'm on the coach and then listen to whatever goes on in the changing room. I'll have a chat with some of the boys too and try to relax. I don't really pick what music is played but occasionally I try to sneak something on. Actually, I got my hands on it after we beat Tottenham last season and had a bit of a dance, which Welbz found quite funny! The song? That was Cola by Camelphat.

Sead Kolasinac: Before we go into the dressing room I'll listen to some music on my headphones. But once we get into the dressing room we all listen to music together. About 20 minutes before the game I get myself mentally ready for it. Before we go out to warm up I'll have some treatment too.

What's the most inspirational speech you can remember?

Petr Cech: I have to say when you play as many games as I've played, and as many big games, there are always moments where people come up with great speeches and great ideas. There were a few over the years and it's very hard to pick one. But you always try to find the way to motivate everybody around you and you try to motivate people to remember why we do what we do and what we want to achieve. You can always feel if somebody hits the nail on the head.

Rob Holding: When I was on loan at Bury, we got promoted from League Two to League One. David Flitcroft was the manager and he talked about Mount Everest, the death zone and how hard it was to survive there because of limited oxygen. He compared it to the league and the last five games in which we needed points to get automatic promotion. We ended up doing it, so that was probably the most motivational one I've had.

Alex Iwobi: In the youth teams there were times Neil Banfield gave speeches and they were all about who you represent – and that at all times, off the pitch as well as on the pitch, you have to remember that.

Hector Bellerin: Before the 2017 FA Cup final the boss gave a very meaningful and emotional speech. You know how much it means to him. There was a lot of external criticism of him and in finals, like that one against Chelsea, he was getting into our heads, telling us we could do it, that we had the potential. He told us what a good team we are, and that if we played our football the game would be ours. That's the way it was. That emotion and the meaning in those words really stuck in our heads and we went on to lift the cup.

What's the worst telling off you have received in a dressing room?

Alex Iwobi: I haven't had a telling off in the first team yet! But I remember with the under-18s I had a poor game and Liam Brady was like, "Look at the size of you! And you're getting bullied!" That's probably the worst I've ever received.

Sead Kolsinac: I can remember it really well. I was playing for Schalke against Bayern Munich and we were down 5-0 at half time. The words at half time weren't that nice to hear, but they sort of worked – we only conceded one in the second half! I don't think many of us will forget that quickly.

Rob Holding: It was at Bolton with Neil Lennon and we were at Elland Road. We were 1-0 down at half-time and he ended up throwing the tactics board across the changing room. It got a reaction out of us, he got us going and firing for the second half.

Have you ever lost your temper in the dressing room?

Nacho Monreal: After the league game against Watford in 2016/17. It was awful. I was furious because we lost three really important points. I remember that I was really, really angry after the game.

Sead Kolasinac: Of course, quite often. But that's normal. You get back into the dressing room after a defeat and everyone is unhappy. Sometimes you can lose your temper in those situations.

Which famous people have visited the Arsenal dressing room?

Rob Holding: I met Tony Adams before a game once, and that was good. It was nice to speak to him for a bit. We always have Robert Pires around at training, which is unbelievable. I have a good laugh with him. Thierry Henry's come in a couple of times too. Beef Johnston the golfer comes in a lot with Rambo, so I've met him as well.

Describe the Arsenal dressing room in three words?

Nacho Monreal: Focused, funny and committed.

Petr Cech: That's a tough one, because it depends on games. If you win an FA Cup then it's a totally different atmosphere to winning a league game. Honestly, I don't know how to do it in just three words!

Hector Bellerin: Friendly, solidarity, team. We're a team, everyone is behind each other in every single situation, and that's what matters.

SOCIAL CLUB

Do you follow our players on Instagram? Here's what they were posting last season.

@m1o_official
She knows which football teams to support 😎⛈️👍 @badgalriri #Rihanna #YaGunnersYa #aftermatchmeeting #worldcup2014 #luckycharm @Arsenal @dfb_team
February 3, 2018

@aubameyang97
#lasthomegame5-0 ⚽⚽ goals 1assist and my boys to say #merciarsene #greatday #aubameyang #A⚡
May 7, 2018

@lacazettealex
More kids it's possible? 😏😂 @juniorgunners #afcmembersday #arsenal ⚫
August 4, 2017

@granitxhaka
I just want to say a big thank you for the support we get in good times and bad times. I feel very blessed and thankful #WeAreTheArsenal ⚫ #GX29 #alwaystogether
February 6, 2018

@nachomonreal_
When the FOX met the GOAT 🐐🦊😂
November 19, 2017

@elnennym
❄️
February 28, 2018

24

@hectorbellerin
After the Palace away game I saw a pic online of a young fan showing her love for me. So I posted on social media to help me find her. It worked!! I went and surprised the family with a visit to their home. Thank you everyone who got involved to make this happen ♥
March 9, 2018

@aaronramsey
Warm down after the game #myboy 🖤
April 22, 2018

@dannywelbeck
Had a lot of fun surprising these young Gooners the other day with a kick about on their new football pitch that was funded by @AFC_Foundation #NightToInspire. Also Good luck to Eliza on her trials for the under 12's girls team 😇
May 12, 2018

@micki_taryan
Was great to attend my first charity dinner with @arsenal ✌️ Thank you @arsenal_foundation #NightToInspire
May 11, 2018

@Petrcech
My ice hockey and @nhl collection is getting bigger. Thank you @hank3onyr for the early present!
👍🎄📖
December 9, 2017

@rholding95
Decent day out with the family at the @NFLUK game today! Vikings with that big win! #OnlyInTheNFL 🏈
October 29, 2017

SPOT THE DIFFERENCE

See if you can spot the 10 differences between these two pictures.

Answers on p61.

FOR THE RECORD

1. Arsenal hold the record for the all-time longest run in league football (49 games), but whose old record did we break?

2. We hold the record for most FA Cup wins. How many?

3. True or false, Petr Cech has kept more clean sheets in the Premier league than any other goalkeeper?

4. What did Arsenal do in 55 consecutive games between 2001 and 2002 to set a new English football record?

5. In 1930 Arsenal and Leicester City played in the highest scoring draw in English football. What was the score?

6. Which legendary Arsenal striker scored a record seven goals in one game against Aston Villa in 1935?

7. What took Nicklas Bendtner a record six seconds to do in the north London derby in December 2007?

8. Before Thierry Henry, who was Arsenal's record goalscorer?

9. Who is the youngest player ever to appear for Arsenal?

10. David O'Leary played more often for Arsenal than any other player – how many times? 722, 822 or 922?

11. Thierry Henry set a record for scoring at least 20 goals in how many consecutive Premier League seasons?

12. In which season did Arsenal set a record 10 consecutive clean sheets in the Champions League?

13. What record did Jens Lehmann set in 2011?

14. Against which team did Thierry Henry break the all-time Arsenal goalscoring record?

15. Mesut Ozil became the fastest player to reach 50 what in 2017/18?

Answers on p61.

ARSENAL AT THE WORLD CUP

Arsenal had nine players at the 2018 World Cup finals in Russia, all hoping to join the exclusive club of six men who won football's biggest prize while representing the Gunners.

In the end only one player, Danny Welbeck, made it further than the Round of 16, and he featured just once for Gareth Southgate's England side.

Lucas Torreira played for Uruguay, but didn't join the Gunners until after they exited the tournament.

Here's how the other nine got on during the summer...

Colombia
David Ospina

Ospina's World Cup run was ended by England in the Round of 16, though he did save one penalty in the shootout. The goalkeeper had earlier kept clean sheets against Poland and Senegal in the group stage, to help Colombia finish second in Group H. He made 10 saves in the tournament, and was only beaten from the penalty spot in the defeat to England.

England
Danny Welbeck

Welbeck only came on for one appearance for England, as a late sub in the final group game against Belgium. England had already qualified before that 1-0 defeat, and Welbeck was a spectator as the Three Lions saw off Colombia (on penalties) and Sweden (2-0) in the knock out stage, before losing 2-1 to Croatia in the semi-final. Welbeck was an unused sub again as England lost the third place play-off 2-0 to Belgium.

Switzerland
Stephan
Lichtsteiner and
Granit Xhaka

Switzerland national team captain Lichtsteiner joined Arsenal from Juventus shortly before the start of the tournament, and played all three group games, helping the Swiss finish second in Group E behind Brazil. He was suspended for the Round of 16 defeat to Sweden. Xhaka however was ever-present in the midfield, and scored a fantastic goal in the group stage win over Serbia. In fact Xhaka played all 360 minutes of their campaign, also helping Switzerland to draws with Brazil and Costa Rica.

Germany
Mesut Ozil

Ozil was hoping to repeat his achievement of four years ago, when he was an instrumental part of Germany's World Cup success in Brazil. But it wasn't to be for the Gunners' attacking midfielder this time around, as the Germans failed to even make it past the group stage. Ozil played in the 1-0 defeat to Mexico and also the 2-0 reverse to South Korea in the final game that sealed their fate. He did however create no fewer than seven goalscoring chances from open play in that last match, more than any other player managed during the group stages.

Spain
Nacho
Monreal

The left back was selected as part of Spain's squad, but didn't make it onto the pitch in any of their four games as they surprisingly lost to hosts Russia on penalties in the Round of 16.

Nigeria
Alex Iwobi

Experiencing his first ever World Cup finals, Iwobi featured in all three group games for Nigeria, who finished third in Group D. The young forward started the 2-0 defeat to Croatia, then was used from the bench in the 2-0 win over Iceland and also the late defeat to Argentina in the final game that knocked the Super Eagles out of the tournament.

Costa Rica
Joel Campbell

One of his country's most capped players of all time, Campbell – who has since left Arsenal – played twice in the group stage for Costa Rica, claiming an assist in the 2-2 draw against Switzerland. He also started the 1-0 defeat to Serbia, but was surprisingly omitted from the 2-0 loss against Brazil. Costa Rica, who reached the quarter-finals in Brazil in 2014, finished bottom of Group E this time around.

Egypt
Mohamed Elneny

A mainstay of the Egypt midfield, Elneny played in all three group games, but couldn't help his country reach the knockout stages. They lost all three matches, going down to Uruguay 1-0, hosts Russia 3-1 and Saudi Arabia 2-1 to finish bottom of Group A.

Arsenal have had six winners of the World Cup in the past, more than any other English club side.

1998 - France
Patrick Vieira and Emmanuel Petit

2010 - Spain
Cesc Fabregas

2014 - Germany
Lukas Podolski, Mesut Ozil and Per Mertesacker

WONDERFUL WORLD OF ARSENAL

What's in a name? Here's a selection of weird and wonderful facts about the various names that have played for Arsenal down the years.

Throughout history, there has been at least one Arsenal player whose surname begins with each letter of the alphabet, from Tony Adams to Gedion Zelalem.

Edu, at just three characters, was the shortest name to play for us, though his full name is Eduardo Cesar Daude Gaspar. Defender Ian Ure had just six characters in his whole name.

At 24 characters, new signing Sokratis Papastathopoulos is the longest name to play for Arsenal (not including middle names). Pierre-Emerick Aubameyang is second with 23 characters, defender Konstantinos Mavropanos has 22.

Freddie Ljungberg is actually Karl Ljungberg, Freddie is his middle name.

The most common first name to play for Arsenal is James (or Jimmy) with 48 players so far.

The most common surname among Arsenal players is Shaw (seven).

Former Arsenal youth player Ilias Chatzitheodoridis has 10 syllables in his name – more than any other Gunners player.

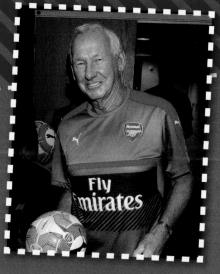

Ten Arsenal players have been known by just one name – Eduardo, Gilberto, Edu, Kanu, Gabriel, Lauren, Juan, Silvinho, Denilson and Gervinho.

Bob Wilson's middle name is Primrose, while David Jack – striker from the 1930s – had the middle name Bone Nightingale.

Three Campbells have played for Arsenal in the Premier League – Sol, Joel and Kevin.

Players with double-barrelled surnames to play for Arsenal: Oxlade-Chamberlain, Maitland-Niles, Emmanuel-Thomas, Reine-Adelaide and Owusu-Abeyie.

In 2009 Arsenal gave a first-team debut to a certain Tom Cruise. Our Mr Cruise was a left back though, not a film star.

Two Alan Smiths played for Arsenal – one who played three times in 1946 and the more famous one who played 347 times in the 1980s and 90s.

Danny Welbeck's full name is Daniel Nii Tackie Mensah Welbeck.

Former Arsenal midfielder Marcus McGuane began his career as Marcus Agyei-Tabi.

We know the full names of all 857 players to have represented the Arsenal first team – except one. The mysterious R Foster, who played twice in 1889.

Tim Coleman – who played 196 times in the early 20th century, was actually called John Coleman, but gained the nickname Tim as that is how he addressed everyone whose name he did not know or couldn't remember!

Arsenal – the most successful women's football club in the country – celebrated their 30th anniversary in 2017/18.

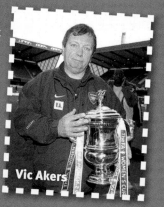

Vic Akers

The club was founded in 1987 by former manager Vic Akers, who revolutionised the women's game in this country during his 22 years in charge.

He led the side to an incredible 33 trophies during that time, all starting with a League Cup success in 1992. That was followed with a domestic treble the following season, and he went on to win 11 league titles in all, 10 FA Cups and 10 League Cups. But the crowning glory came in 2007, when Arsenal became champions of Europe, beating Swedish side Umea in the final thanks to Alex Scott's late winner. It remains the only time any English women's team has conquered the continent.

This achievement came on top of completing a remarkable unbeaten domestic campaign that year, in which Arsenal won all 22 league fixtures, scoring 119 goals in the process.

Akers stepped down in 2009, and since his departure the club have added three more league titles, four FA Cups and five WSL Cups.

Still firmly established among the leading sides in the FA Women's Super League, the Gunners are now under the management of Australian boss Joe Montemurro, and the side features exciting talent such as Leah Williamson, Danielle van de Donk, Kim Little and Vivianne Miedema.

Home matches are played at Meadow Park, home of Football Conference side Boreham Wood FC, in Hertfordshire and hopes are high that the team can add to their impressive, record-breaking trophy haul this season.

ARSENAL WOMEN FC MAJOR HONOURS

League champions (14)

1992/93, 1994/95, 1996/97, 2000/01, 2001/02, 2003/04, 2004/05, 2005/06, 2006/07, 2007/08, 2008/09, 2009/10, 2010/11, 2011/12

FA Women's Cup (14)

1992/93, 1994/95, 1997/98, 1998/99, 2000/01, 2003/04, 2005/06, 2006/07, 2007/08, 2008/09, 2010/11, 2012/13, 2013/14, 2015/16

Women's League Cup (15)

1991/92, 1992/93, 1993/94, 1997/98, 1998/99, 1999/2000, 2000/01, 2004/05, 2006/07, 2008/09, 2010/11, 2011/12, 2012/13, 2014/15, 2017/18

Women's Champions League (1)

2006/07

Joe Montemurro and Jordan Nobbs

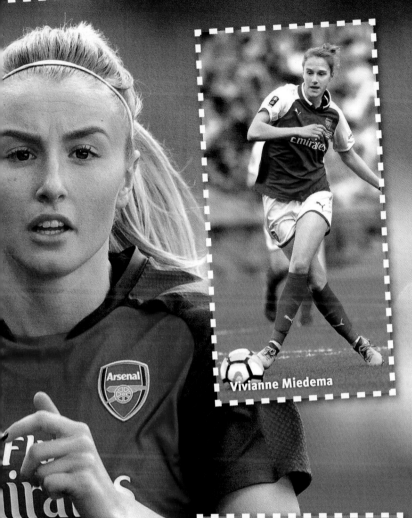

Vivianne Miedema

LEGENDARY PLAYERS

TOP 10 APPEARANCE-MAKERS

Emma Byrne	459
Ciara Grant	403
Jayne Ludlow	356
Rachel Yankey	314
Alex Scott	313
Faye White	227
Gemma Davison	214
Lianne Sanderson	184
Katie Chapman	181
Danielle Carter	178

TOP 10 GOALSCORERS

Jayne Ludlow	211
Lianne Sanderson	139
Angela Banks	133
Kelly Smith	130
Julie Fleeting	130
Kim Little	113
Ciara Grant	102
Rachel Yankey	102
Marieanne Spacey	79
Danielle Carter	60

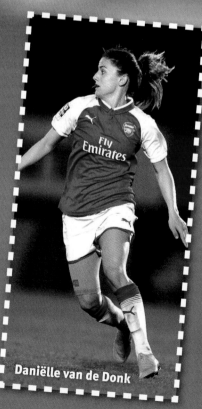

Daniëlle van de Donk

Leah Williamson

PLAYER PROFILES

GOALKEEPERS

Petr Cech #1

The goalkeeper with the most clean sheets in Premier League history, Petr is the most experienced and most decorated member of the squad. A Champions League winner with previous club Chelsea, he won the Community Shield on his debut, and lifted the FA Cup in 2017. The most capped Czech international of all time, he passed 100 Arsenal appearances last season, and also recorded his 200th Premier League clean sheet, after saving a penalty against Watford at Emirates Stadium. The nine-time Czech Footballer of the year is a natural leader and communicator on the pitch and in the dressing room.

Born: Pilsen, Czech Republic, May 20, 1982
Joined Arsenal: from Chelsea on June 29, 2015
Previous clubs: Chmel Blsany, Sparta Prague, Rennes, Chelsea
Arsenal debut: v Chelsea (n) Community Shield, Aug 2, 2015

Emiliano Martinez #26

Argentina youth international Emi is now into his seventh season at Arsenal, though much of that time has been spent out on loan. He played for Getafe in Spain's La Liga last term, though was restricted to just five appearances. He previously enjoyed an excellent loan spell at Wolves in the Championship in 2015/16, and returned to the Gunners the following season to make five appearances for the first team, keeping three clean sheets. A modern-style goalkeeper with excellent distribution, Emi was just 17 when he moved to Arsenal from hometown club Independiente.

Born: Buenos Aires, Argentina, Sept 2, 1992
Joined Arsenal: from Independiente on Aug 1, 2010
Previous clubs: Independiente, Oxford Utd (loan), Sheff Wed (loan), Rotherham Utd (loan), Wolves (loan)
Arsenal debut: v Coventry City (h), League Cup, Sept 26, 2012

Hector Bellerin #2

Since breaking through as a youngster in 2014/15, Hector has gone on to become one of the most highly regarded right backs in European football. The Spaniard joined from home town club Barcelona when he was just 16, and now has more than 150 first-team appearances to his name. Incredibly fast and dangerous going forward, Hector can also play at right wingback, and contributed three goals last season, including a valuable late equaliser at home to Chelsea. A senior international with Spain since 2016, he was named in the PFA Premier League Team of the Season in 2015/16.

Born: Barcelona, Spain, Mar 19, 1995
Joined Arsenal: as a scholar in summer 2011
Previous club: Watford (loan)
Arsenal debut: v West Brom (a), League Cup, Sept 25, 2013

Laurent Koscielny #6

Long-serving and dependable centre back Laurent has racked up more than 300 appearances for the first team since arriving, virtually unknown, from France in 2010. In that time he has established himself as a mainstay at the heart of the defence for both club and country, with more than 50 caps for the France national team. The club's highest scoring defender in the Premier League era, Laurent is a strong, physical, intelligent defender who often took the captain's armband last season. This is his ninth season at the club, though he is expected to miss the first half of it with an Achilles injury suffered in the Europa League semi-final last term.

Born: Tulle, France, Sept 10, 1985
Joined Arsenal: from Lorient on July 2, 2010
Previous clubs: Guingamp, Tours, Lorient
Arsenal debut: v Liverpool (a) League, Aug 15, 2010

Rob Holding #16

Now into his third season at Arsenal, England Under-21 international defender Rob signed a new long-term contract with the club at the end of last season. Formerly with Bolton Wanderers, he was snapped up in summer 2016 and particularly excelled in the FA Cup triumph over Chelsea in his debut season. Now with more than 50 appearances to his name, the athletic central defender continues to develop into a reliable member of the Gunners backline, and scored his first goal for the club last season, during the Europa League group stage win away to BATE Borisov.

Born: Tameside, Sept 20, 1995
Joined Arsenal: from Bolton Wanderers on July 22, 2016
Previous clubs: Bolton Wanderers, Bury (loan)
Arsenal debut: v Liverpool (h) League, Aug 14, 2016

Nacho Monreal #18

A contender for Arsenal Player of the Season last year, Nacho sets consistently high standards at left back, and has also matured into an accomplished central defender recently. Signed midway through the 2012/13 season, the Spain international has rarely been out of the side since, and last term added goalscoring to his considerable list of attributes, netting six in all competitions – twice as many as he managed in his previous five seasons combined. Three times an FA Cup winner with the Gunners, he was part of his country's World Cup squad in Russia this summer, having previously helped Spain to the final of the 2013 Confederations Cup.

Born: Pamplona, Spain, Feb 26, 1986
Joined Arsenal: from Malaga on Jan 31, 2013
Previous clubs: Osasuna, Malaga
Arsenal debut: v Stoke City (h) League, Feb 2, 2013

Shkodran Mustafi #20

A World Cup winner with Germany in 2014, central defender Shkodran is now in his third season at the club, after making a big-money move from Spanish club Valencia. Previously on the books of Everton as a youngster, the wholehearted centre back then impressed in Italy for Sampdoria, before enjoying two successful seasons in Spain. He endeared himself to Arsenal fans last term with a goal in the north London derby win over Tottenham at Emirates Stadium, and also netted in wins over Crystal Palace and Watford. He remained unbeaten for the first 22 games of his Gunners career after making his debut in 2016.

Born: Bad Hersfeld, Germany, Apr 17, 1992
Joined Arsenal: from Valencia on Aug 29, 2016
Previous clubs: Everton, Sampdoria, Valencia
Arsenal debut: v Southampton (h) League, Sept 10, 2016

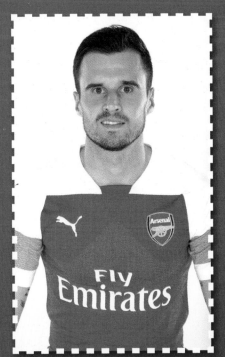

Carl Jenkinson #25

Boyhood Arsenal fan Carl spent last season on loan at Birmingham City in the Championship, but injury restricted him to just seven appearances for the Blues. The right back signed for Arsenal in 2011, and scored his first goal for the club at the end of his third season, against Norwich on the final day of the campaign. A successful two-year loan spell at West Ham followed, though it ended with a cruciate ligament injury. A hardworking, tireless full back capable of delivering an excellent cross, he was capped by England in late 2012, having played for Finland at youth level.

Born: Harlow, Feb 8, 1992
Joined Arsenal: from Charlton Athletic on June 8, 2011
Previous clubs: Charlton Athletic, Eastbourne Borough (loan), Welling United (loan), West Ham United (loan)
Arsenal debut: v Udinese (h) Champions League, Aug 16, 2011

Konstantinos Mavropanos #27

Joining from the Greek League halfway through last season, Konstantinos had to wait until the final weeks of the campaign to make his debut, but impressed during his first-team bow at Old Trafford. After another accomplished display at home to Burnley, he was sent off in his third outing at Leicester but had already shown plenty of promise in his initial outings in red and white. Known around the club as Dinos, the powerful, tall central defender is a Greece under-21 international who excelled during the pre-season tour to Singapore in the summer.

Born: Athens, Greece, Dec 11, 1997
Joined Arsenal: from PAS Giannina on Jan 4, 2018
Previous club: PAS Giannina
Arsenal debut: v Man United (a) League, Apr 29, 2018

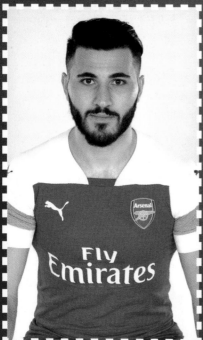

Sead Kolasinac #31

Sead became the first player in eight years to score on his Arsenal debut when he headed the equaliser in last season's Community Shield triumph over Chelsea. Most at home as a left-sided wingback, Sead can also operate at left back, and impressed during his first season with his fully-committed, barrelling style – powering forward at every opportunity. The Bosnia and Herzegovina international scored five times in all last term, and contributed four assists, winning the Arsenal Player of the Month award in both August and October 2017. Physically imposing, he was named in the Bundesliga 2016/17 Team of the Season before joining Arsenal from FC Schalke.

Born: Karlsruhe, Germany, June 20, 1993
Joined Arsenal: from FC Schalke 04 on June 6, 2017
Previous club: FC Schalke 04
Arsenal debut: v Chelsea (n) Community Shield, Aug 8, 2017

Mohamed Elneny #4

An energetic, composed presence in the centre of midfield, Mo proved his value to the Gunners again last season, particularly in European competition where the Egyptian put in several excellent performances. He scored his first goal at Emirates Stadium in the Europa League group stage win over BATE Borisov and also impressed away to Ostersunds and CSKA Moscow particularly. The winner of four Swiss League titles with previous club FC Basel, he rounded off his debut season at the Gunners by winning the Arsenal.com Goal of the Season for his strike against Barcelona. In March 2018 he signed a new long-term contract with the club, then featured for Egypt at the 2018 World Cup in Russia.

Born: El-Mahalla El-Kubra, Egypt, July 11, 1992
Joined Arsenal: from Basel on Jan 14, 2016
Previous clubs: El Mokawloon, Basel
Arsenal debut: v Burnley (h) FA Cup, Jan 30, 2016

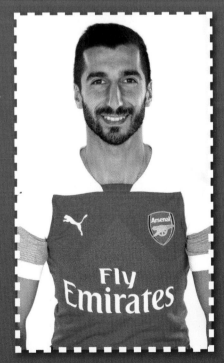

Henrikh Mkhitaryan #7

Armenian playmaker Henrikh wasted no time making a positive impact at the club after his player exchange deal with Alexis Sanchez midway through last season. Having joined from Manchester United in January, he soon linked up with fellow new signing and former Borussia Dortmund team-mate Pierre-Emerick Aubameyang, and contributed a hat-trick of assists at home to Everton. He netted his first goal away to AC Milan, and also scored on his return to Old Trafford, as well as at home to Watford to record three goals and six assists in his first season. A full international for more than 10 years, he has been named Armenian Footballer of the Year eight times.

Born: Yerevan, Armenia, Jan 21, 1989
Joined Arsenal: from Man United on Jan 22, 2018
Previous clubs: Pyunik, Metalurh Donetsk, Shakhtar Donetsk, Borussia Dortmund, Man United
Arsenal debut: v Swansea City (a) League, Jan 30, 2018

Aaron Ramsey #8

With more appearances and goals for the club than any other current member of the first-team squad, Aaron is an influential and crucial part of the team, bringing his dynamism, stamina and creativity to central midfield. The Wales international arrived from boyhood club Cardiff City aged 17, and has since gone on to score the winning goal in two FA Cup finals (2014 and 2017) as well as pass 300 appearances and 50 goals overall for the Gunners. A natural leader on the pitch, with a wholehearted and fully committed playing style, Aaron signed a new long-term contract with the club in summer 2018.

Born: Caerphilly, Wales, Dec 26, 1990
Joined Arsenal: from Cardiff City on June 13, 2008
Previous clubs: Cardiff City, Nottingham Forest (loan), Cardiff City (loan)
Arsenal debut: v FC Twente (a) Champions League, Aug 13, 2008

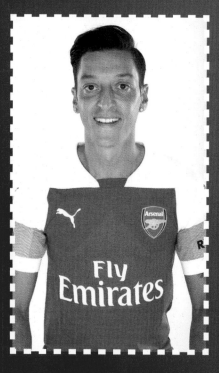

Mesut Ozil #10

One of the most technically gifted creators in European football, Mesut committed his future to the club last season, shortly before breaking another assist record. He racked up his 50th Premier League assist on his 141st appearance in the competition, reaching the landmark faster than any other player in Premier League history. Now in his sixth season at the club, he was named Arsenal Player of the Year in 2016, and won the FA Cup three times in his first four seasons. The attacking midfielder had won the Spanish league title at previous club Real Madrid in 2012 and continually topped the assist charts during three seasons in the Spanish capital. A World Cup winner with Germany in 2014, he appeared at his fifth major international tournament when he featured for his country at Russia 2018, but retired from the national team in the summer.

Born: Gelsenkirchen, Germany, Oct 15, 1988
Joined Arsenal: from Real Madrid on Sept 2, 2013
Previous clubs: Schalke, Werder Bremen, Real Madrid
Arsenal debut: v Sunderland (a) League, Sept 14, 2013

Ainsley Maitland-Niles #15

A product of the Arsenal Academy, central midfielder Ainsley enjoyed a breakthrough season last term, and was rewarded with a new long-term contract in the summer of 2018. Often used at wingback last season, he is more comfortable in the heart of the midfield, as he demonstrated with a superb man of the match display away to Manchester United late in 2017/18. He made nearly 30 appearances in all competitions, continuing the excellent progress he has made ever since joining the Gunners at the age of just six. An England youth international at every age group from under-17 to under-21 level, he won the FIFA Under-20 World Cup in 2017. He enjoyed a productive year on loan to Ipswich Town in the Championship in 2015/16.

Born: Goodmayes, Aug 29, 1997
Joined Arsenal: as a scholar in summer 2013
Previous club: Ipswich Town (loan)
Arsenal debut: v Galatasaray (a) Champions League, Dec 9, 2014

Granit Xhaka #34

An excellent passer of the ball who often operates from deep in Arsenal's central midfield, Granit was ever-present in the Premier League last season. Now in his third season at the club, the Switzerland international is a fearsome tackler who also possesses a thunderous left-foot shot, which he demonstrated with long-range goals in each of his first two seasons in London. Formerly the captain of Borussia Monchengladbach in Germany, Granit signed a new long-term contract with Arsenal in the summer of 2018, shortly before starring for the Swiss national team at the 2018 World Cup in Russia.

Born: Basel, Switzerland, Sept 27, 1992
Joined Arsenal: from Borussia Monchengladbach on May 25, 2016
Previous clubs: Basel, Borussia Monchengladbach
Arsenal debut: v Liverpool (h) League, Aug 14, 2016

PLAYER PROFILES

Alexandre Lacazette #9

Prolific centre forward Alexandre top-scored for the Gunners in his debut season, netting 17 goals in all competitions. The France international joined from Lyon last summer, where he had scored more than 100 times in the French top flight, and registered just seconds into his Premier League debut in August 2017. A natural finisher who can also link the play well, Alexandre scored in every month of the season before picking up an injury in February. He returned in April to score eight times in his final 10 outings.

Born: Lyon, France, May 28, 1991
Joined Arsenal: from Lyon on July 5, 2017
Previous club: Lyon
Arsenal debut: v Chelsea (n) Community Shield, Aug 6, 2017

Pierre-Emerick Aubameyang #14

Arsenal smashed their transfer record to sign exciting striker Pierre-Emerick from Borussia Dortmund in January 2018. The French-born Gabon international striker hit the ground running, scoring on his debut and finishing the season with 10 goals from just 13 starts. A star turn with previous side Dortmund, he scored 141 goals from 213 outings in four and a half seasons with the Bundesliga club. A flamboyant and extrovert character off the pitch, he brings an electric pace to Arsenal's forward play, and is dangerous either on the left wing or in a central attacking role. He is Gabon's all-time leading goalscorer, despite starting his international career with the France youth teams.

Born: Laval, France, June 18, 1989
Joined Arsenal: from Borussia Dortmund on Jan 31, 2018
Previous clubs: AC Milan, Dijon (loan), Lille (loan), Monaco (loan), Saint-Etienne, Borussia Dortmund
Arsenal debut: v Everton (h) Premier League, Feb 3, 2018

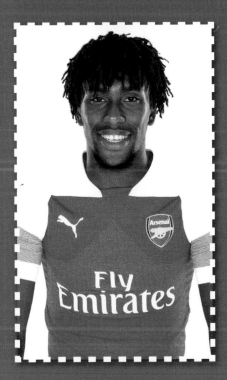

Alex Iwobi #17

A product of the Arsenal Academy, Alex continued his impressive development last season, featuring 39 times in all competitions. Since making his first-team debut aged 19 in 2015, the versatile forward has proved to be a valuable member of the squad, impressing with his creativity and work ethic. An Arsenal player from the age of eight, Alex has an abundance of natural skill and technique, and is at home on either flank. Nephew of Nigeria legend Jay-Jay Okocha, Alex represented the Super Eagles at the 2018 World Cup in Russia.

Born: Lagos, Nigeria, May 3, 1996
Joined Arsenal: as a scholar in summer 2012
Arsenal debut: v Sheff Wed (a) League Cup, Oct 27, 2015

Danny Welbeck #23

An all-action, physical and quick forward, Danny often starts in wide positions, but is always dangerous when running at goal. He reached double figures for goals last season, from 43 appearances, in what was his fourth campaign since joining from boyhood club Manchester United. He won the Premier League title with United, as well as the FIFA World Club Cup, and scored the goal for Arsenal that knocked his old club out of the competition en route to winning the 2015 FA Cup. A regular England international since 2011, he was part of Gareth Southgate's squad at the 2018 World Cup.

Born: Manchester, Nov 26, 1990
Joined Arsenal: from Manchester United on Sept 2, 2014
Previous clubs: Man Utd, Preston NE (loan), Sunderland (loan)
Arsenal debut: v Man City (h) League, Sept 13, 2014

NEW SIGNINGS

Sokratis Papastathopoulos #5

Powerful central defender Sokratis joined from Bundesliga high-fliers Borussia Dortmund, where he had spent five highly productive seasons.

The experienced Greece international won the German Cup and Super Cup (twice) during his time in Dortmund, where he was a team-mate of both Henrikh Mkhitaryan and Pierre-Emerick Aubameyang.

Voted Best Greek Young Player in 2007/08, Sokratis left AEK Athens in 2008 and had spells with Genoa and AC Milan in Italy before moving to Germany. Initially with Werder Bremen, he joined Dortmund in 2013, impressing in his debut season and being named in the Bundesliga Team of 2013/14.

A solid, no-nonsense defender with inbuilt leadership qualities, he represented his country at Euro 2012 and the 2014 World Cup finals in Brazil.

Defender
Born: Kalamata, Greece, June 9, 1988
Joined Arsenal: from Borussia Dortmund on July 2, 2018

Stephan Lichtsteiner #12

Right back Stephan was Unai Emery's first signing of the summer, arriving from Italian giants Juventus where he had won seven league titles in succession. A vastly experienced defender, and captain of the Switzerland national team, Stephan is a natural leader, with boundless energy. Capable of steaming forward in a right wing role, or as a full back in part of a back four, he showed Arsenal fans his combative nature during the World Cup in Russia, helping the Swiss out of a tricky looking group.

Previously with Lazio (where he won the Coppa Italia in 2009) and Grasshoppers of Zurich (winning the Swiss championship in 2002/03), he was named Swiss Footballer of the Year in 2015. He has won more than 100 caps for his country, after making 30 appearances for the under-21s.

He joined Arsenal on a free transfer, after his contract with Juventus expired.

Defender
Born: Adligenswil, Switzerland, January 16, 1984
Joined Arsenal: from Juventus on June 5, 2018

Bernd Leno #19

Germany international goalkeeper Bernd arrived from Bundesliga side Bayer Leverkusen after narrowly missing out on selection for the World Cup.

He had spent seven seasons with Leverkusen, playing more than 300 times for the club he joined as a teenager from Stuttgart. He built a reputation as a penalty specialist there, saving six spot kicks in the 2013/14 season alone, and also impressed with the ball at his feet, happy to play the ball out from defence under pressure. Quick off his line and athletic, the German also has excellent reflexes.

Having represented Germany at every youth level from under-17 to under-21, Bernd made his senior debut in 2016 and was part of the squad that won the Confederations Cup in 2017, playing in the group stage win over Australia. He had earlier won the European Under-17s Championships in 2009.

Goalkeeper
Born: Bietigheim-Bissingen, Germany, March 4, 1992
Joined Arsenal: from Bayer Leverkusen on June 19, 2018

Lucas Torreira #11

Combative, tireless midfielder Lucas signed for the Gunners after impressing at the World Cup with Uruguay. Having only made his senior international debut at the start of 2018, he played in all five games for his country in Russia, helping them to the quarter-finals.

Though short in stature, the youngster is a tough tackler who also delivers excellent set pieces. He spent two seasons in central midfield at Sampdoria in Italy's Serie A before moving to London, having previously been with fellow Italian side Pescara, who he joined as a teenager.

Born in Fray Bentos in Uruguay, Lucas is a highly committed defensive midfielder with undoubted potential and an excellent work ethic.

Midfielder
Born: Fray Bentos, Uruguay, February 11, 1996
Joined Arsenal: from Sampdoria on July 10, 2018

Matteo Guendouzi #29

Little-known French teenager Matteo joined the Gunners in pre-season from Ligue 2 side Lorient. A France youth international at under-18, under-19 and under-20 levels, the frizzy-haired midfielder started his career in the youth section at Paris Saint-Germain before moving to Lorient. He made his league debut for them at the start of 2016/17, aged just 17. But it was last season when he made an eye-catching breakthrough, playing more than 25 times for the club and attracting the attention of the Gunners scouts. A player who is comfortable on the ball with an excellent passing range, Matteo also has a fierce determination and competitive spirit.

Midfielder
Born: Poissy, France, April 14, 1999
Joined Arsenal: from Lorient on July 11, 2018

UNAI EMERY

As well as five new signings, Arsenal also welcomed a new man in charge – for the first time for 22 years.

Spaniard Unai Emery was named as head coach in late May, after Arsène Wenger's 1,235-game reign came to an end.

Emery joined from Paris Saint-Germain, where he won an incredible seven trophies in just two years in charge, including the domestic quadruple of league title, French Cup, French League Cup and the Ligue 1 equivalent of the Community Shield. He won 87 of his 114 games in the French capital.

Previously he had been manager of Sevilla in Spain, where he became the first man to ever win the Europa League three seasons in a row, lifting the trophy in 2014, 2015 and 2016 (when he beat Liverpool in the final).

Before that he had managed Spartak Moscow, Valencia, Almeria and Lorca Deportivo.

A midfielder in his playing days, his whole career was spent in his home country, starting at Real Sociedad.

As a coach Emery is known as a master tactician, with a keen analytical eye and emphasis on hard work and organisation.

Aged 46 when he took over at Arsenal, Emery favours an attractive style of play, and likes his players to win back possession as soon as possible after losing it.

"I am honoured to be here – there's no better club than Arsenal," Emery said when taking over. "From the first meetings I had with Arsenal, I had a very good feeling about working together and that we could create a new present and future Arsenal.

"I want to thank Arsène Wenger for his legacy. For all the coaches over the world he's a reference and I learned so many things in football from him. My English is not very good now and I want to make an effort to speak to the supporters, to explain my ideas, to explain my ambitions, to explain that I am very excited about this opportunity. It's a big club, a great city, a grand stadium and also has great players.

"For me, the challenge is a dream come true."

1000 UP!

Arsenal's last match of last season was the club's 1,000th fixture in Premier League history – here we take a look back at some of the more notable among them...

Game number 238

May 3, 1998

Arsenal 4, Everton 0

The game that clinched Arsenal's first-ever Premier League title will forever be remembered for captain Tony Adams's late strike. Slaven Bilic scored an early own goal before a double from Marc Overmars, either side of half-time, put the Gunners firmly in control. Arsenal were cruising to a first league title in seven years, wrapping up the championship with two games to spare, and Adams added the icing on the cake in the last minute. Sent through by central defensive partner Steve Bould, Adams strode forward before unleashing a powerful left-foot shot to make it 4-0. "That sums it all up" was commentator Martin Tyler's assessment – the Gunners had certainly become champions in fine style.

Game number 391

May 8, 2002

Manchester United 0, Arsenal 1

Arsenal wrapped up their second Premier League title at the home of Manchester United, the reigning champions and bitter rivals of the era. Arsène Wenger's men hadn't lost an away game in the league all season going into this game, and had also scored in every single Premier League fixture. They maintained both records at Old Trafford, when Sylvain Wiltord pounced to net the winner on 55 minutes. Just four days earlier the Gunners had beaten Chelsea 2-0 in the FA Cup final, so this victory also completed another double for the club. Arsenal were good value for the win, and it was the away fans at Old Trafford who celebrated long into the night on an unforgettable Premier League occasion.

Game number 468

May 15, 2004

Arsenal 2, Leicester City 1

The club's third Premier League title had already been secured at White Hart Lane, but this win over Leicester City at Highbury on the final day of the season was just as historic. By avoiding defeat, this Arsenal team ensured they would go down in history as the modern era's first 'invincible' side completing – an entire 38-game league programme without losing. The visitors threatened to cause an upset when former Gunner Paul Dickov stole in at the far post to head Leicester ahead, but normal service was resumed in the second half when Thierry Henry equalised from the penalty spot. Then skipper Patrick Vieira took centre stage, running onto Dennis Bergkamp's throughball before rounding the keeper. The final whistle blew, Arsenal's league record read P38 W26 D12 L0 - footballing immortality achieved.

Game number  544

May 7, 2006
Arsenal 4, Wigan Athletic 2

The last ever game staged at Highbury proved monumental. Arsenal needed to better Tottenham's result on the final day to leapfrog their local rivals and take the last Champions League spot. And despite Wigan taking a shock 2-1 lead after Robert Pires had opened the scoring, that's exactly what happened. Predictably, it was largely down to Thierry Henry. The man with more goals in Highbury's 93-year history than anyone else took over proceedings, scoring an incredible hat-trick to kick-start wild celebrations on an emotional afternoon in north London. The stadium was resplendent in red and white – with every supporter given a commemorative tee shirt for the fixture – and the farewell party went to plan. The 38,000 fans present on that historic afternoon were given one more precious Highbury memory to cherish forever.

Game number 760

February 26, 2012
Arsenal 5, Tottenham Hotspur 2

The Gunners were in a certain amount of disarray going into the second north London derby of the season. With just 13 games remaining, Spurs were 10 points ahead of Arsène Wenger's men, and soon raced into a 2-0 lead at Emirates Stadium. Then came the comeback. Bacary Sagna scored a fine header before an excellent strike from Robin van Persie levelled matters at the break. In the second-half Arsenal went into overdrive – Tomas Rosicky put the hosts ahead before Theo Walcott scored twice to complete a memorable rout, and trigger a run of form that would overhaul Tottenham on the final day of the season.

And as if to prove this win was no fluke, Arsenal beat Spurs by exactly the same scoreline in the following season's corresponding fixture.

Game number 1,000

May 14, 2018
Huddersfield Town 0, Arsenal 1

This was Arsène Wenger's last-ever game as manager of Arsenal. He had taken charge of 828 of the club's 1,000 Premier League fixtures, signing off with his 476th win in the competition on the final day of last season, thanks to Pierre-Emerick Aubameyang's first-half strike. The match itself wasn't a classic, rather a celebration of an incredible reign – the longest and most successful in the club's history. It also meant the Frenchman signed off with another record – this was the 48th different stadium at which Wenger enjoyed victory in Premier League history. When the final whistle blew, the manager saluted and embraced the travelling fans in an emotional farewell. He bowed out as the man who had overseen more Premier League games than any other manager.

YOUNG GUNS

The club's young talent fired Arsenal to the Premier League 2 title last season, as well as the finals of the PL International Cup and FA Youth Cup.

These three young forwards were particularly impressive during an excellent season for the Arsenal youth setup, scoring 36 goals between them.

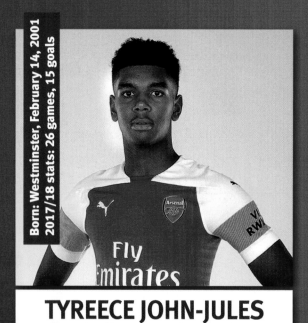

Born: Westminster, February 14, 2001
2017/18 stats: 26 games, 15 goals

TYREECE JOHN-JULES

Finishing, strength and link-up play – three essential qualities for a modern-day striker, and all attributes that Tyreece possesses in abundance.

The exciting centre forward has grown up at Arsenal, joining the club at under-eight level, but it was last season when he really began to make his mark in the big youth competitions – the FA Youth Cup and Premier League 2. In fact he also found the net in the Under-18 Premier Academy League and Premier League International Cup as well, netting 15 goals across all competitions in 2017/18.

He's used to topping the scoring charts though – a natural-born goal-getter, the prolific marksman claimed 30 goals the season before that, while still a schoolboy.

So it was no surprise when the club offered him his first professional contract in February 2018, a few days after his 17th birthday.

Many of his highlights last season came in the FA Youth Cup, and he will long remember his extra-time goal at Anfield to knock out Liverpool in the fourth round.

Like many of the young pros at Arsenal, he is a youth international, and he joined up with Xavier Amaechi in May 2018 to take part in the European Under-17s Championships. He played three times as England reached the semi-final, and although he scored a penalty in the shootout against Holland, the Three Lions crashed out at that stage.

It will undoubtedly have been a learning experience for the youngster though, and he will continue to develop over the coming years, with his natural desire to improve and take on board the coaches' instructions.

Over his decade or so at the Arsenal academy, Tyreece has become genuinely two-footed – working on building his left foot to be as effective as his right – and continues to work on his athleticism, increasing his pace year on year.

Born: Bath, January 5, 2001
2017/18 stats: 25 games, 10 goals

XAVIER AMAECHI

Teenage forward Xavier burst onto the scene last season with five goals in the under-18 team's run to the FA Youth Cup final.

The England youth international scored the consolation goal in the two-legged final defeat to Chelsea, and also netted in the quarter-final and semi-final, proving highly effective up front with his lightning pace and cool finishing. Often operating from the wing, Xavier is comfortable in a variety of attacking positions, and loves to run at defenders.

He joined the Arsenal Academy from Fulham when he was just 12, and was soon playing above his age group. He made his under-18 debut aged just 15.

Last season he was part of the England side that reached the semi-final of the European Under-17 Championships. He played five matches for the Three Lions, scoring in the quarter-final win over Norway, but then missed out on the semi-final defeat to eventual winners Holland through suspension.

Though born in Bath, he is still eligible to represent Nigeria at international level, despite having starred for England youth teams.

He signed his first professional contract with Arsenal in early 2018, on the same day that he turned 17 years old. Shortly afterwards he made the step up to the under-23 team, making his debut at that level midway through the campaign.

If he can repeat that rate of development over the coming seasons, you can be sure we will be hearing a lot more about Xavier very soon.

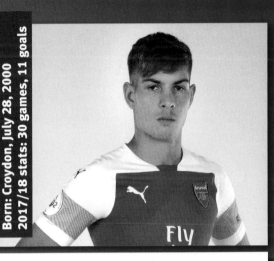

Born: Croydon, July 28, 2000
2017/18 stats: 30 games, 11 goals

EMILE SMITH ROWE

Most comfortable operating in the number 10 role behind the front men, Emile is both a creator and taker of goalscoring chances.

He joined the Gunners youth setup back in 2010, and has steadily worked his way through the ranks since – he was just 16 years old when he made his debut at under-23 level in 2016/17.

Last season was another landmark year for Emile, despite suffering an ankle injury late in the campaign. He had already lit up the campaign with some tremendous goals, not least a curling effort against Sunderland, and an incredible free-kick in the FA Youth Cup against Colchester United.

That was one of four goals for the youngster in that competition last season, but he also played a major part in helping the under-23s win the Premier League 2 title, playing ten times in the championship-winning campaign.

But it should have come as no surprise – Emile was just continuing his form from the previous summer, when he played a major role in England's triumph at the 2017 Under-17 World Cup in India. It was the first time the national team had ever won the highest honour at that age group, and Emile made his mark by setting up one of the goals in the semi-final win over Brazil.

It all means the talented teen is edging ever nearer to the Arsenal first team. In fact last season he was named as the extra man in the squad for the match against Ostersunds at home in the Europa League. It was his first taste of life in the Arsenal dressing room, and we suspect there will be many more in the near future.

WONDERFUL WORLD OF ARSENAL

Everyone knows what the Invincibles team achieved, but we bet you didn't know a few of these facts...

- Arsenal remained unbeaten for a record 49 league games between May 7, 2003 and October 16, 2004 inclusive – spanning three seasons.

- We used 33 different players during the run, Thierry Henry and Kolo Toure both played 48 games out of 49. Henry missed just 98 minutes of the sequence.

- The overall record was P49 W36 D13 L0 F112 A35.

- Arsenal amassed 121 points during the 49 games, at a rate of 2.47 per match.

- There were 15 goalscorers in the run, Henry top-scored with 39, followed by Robert Pires on 23. Five own goals were also scored in our favour. Henry also contributed 19 assists.

- The first game of the run was a 6-1 win over Southampton, in which Jermaine Pennant and Robert Pires scored hat-tricks.

- David Bentley, Stathis Tavlaridis and Ryan Garry each played only one game for Arsenal in the Premier League, for all of them it was the opening game of the unbeaten run.

- Of the 49 games, 25 were at home and 24 away. We conceded just 14 goals in those away matches, compared to 21 at home.

- Arsenal didn't trail in the final 20 minutes of any match during the run. The latest we were behind in any game was after 68 minutes, against Tottenham at home.

- While Arsenal remained unbeaten, England won seven Test matches against the West Indies, ten different countries joined the EU, Southampton had four managers and Britney Spears got married twice.

- Arsenal lost six matches in other competitions during the run. Our longest unbeaten run in all competitions is 27 games, set in 2007.

- The biggest win in the run was 6-1 against Southampton in the first game. We also beat Leeds United 5-0.

- During the unbeaten run Chelsea lost eight league games, Manchester United 10, Liverpool 14, and Tottenham 23.

- David Seaman (aged 39) was the oldest player to appear in the run, Cesc Fabregas (at 17) was the youngest.

- Arsenal picked up three red cards during the run (Sol Campbell, Ashley Cole and Patrick Vieira).

- When Arsenal beat Blackburn 3-0 at home on August 25, 2004 the club overtook Nottingham Forest's previous record of 42 unbeaten league games, set in 1978.

- The run included the whole of the 2003/04 Premier League season, only the second time, after Preston North End in 1888/89, that a side had managed this in English league football.

- Arsenal were awarded a special edition gold version of the Premier League trophy for remaining unbeaten in 2003/04.

- Arsenal played 21 different teams in the run, beating all of them at least once apart from Manchester United and Portsmouth.

WORDSEARCH

All of these players scored at least one penalty for the Gunners, how many can you find?

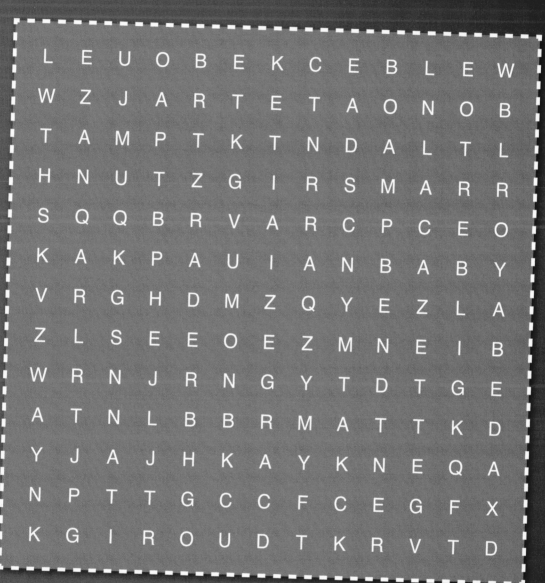

L	E	U	O	B	E	K	C	E	B	L	E	W
W	Z	J	A	R	T	E	T	A	O	N	O	B
T	A	M	P	T	K	T	N	D	A	L	T	L
H	N	U	T	Z	G	I	R	S	M	A	R	R
S	Q	Q	B	R	V	A	R	C	P	C	E	O
K	A	K	P	A	U	I	A	N	B	A	B	Y
V	R	G	H	D	M	Z	Q	Y	E	Z	L	A
Z	L	S	E	E	O	E	Z	M	N	E	I	B
W	R	N	J	R	N	G	Y	T	D	T	G	E
A	T	N	L	B	B	R	M	A	T	T	K	D
Y	J	A	J	H	K	A	Y	K	N	E	Q	A
N	P	T	T	G	C	C	F	C	E	G	F	X
K	G	I	R	O	U	D	T	K	R	V	T	D

Adebayor	**Cazorla**	**Giroud**
Arshavin	**Eboue**	**Henry**
Arteta	**Eduardo**	**Lacazette**
Aubameyang	**Fabregas**	**Nasri**
Bendtner	**Gilberto**	**Welbeck**

Answers on p61.

DESIGN A KIT!

Puma always design some fantastic playing kits for us each season – now it's your turn! Get creative, grab your colouring pens and using Gunnersaurus as your model, see if you can design a brilliant Arsenal kit!

COMPETITION

Answer the following question correctly and you could win an Arsenal FC shirt signed by a first team player.

Who was Arsenal's top scorer last season?

A. Pierre-Emerick Aubameyang
B. Mesut Ozil
C. Alexandre Lacazette

Entry is by email only. Only one entry per contestant. Please enter AFC SHIRT followed by either A, B or C in the subject line of an email. In the body of the email, please include your full name, address, postcode, email address and phone number and send to: frontdesk@grangecommunications.co.uk by Friday 29th March 2019.

Last year's WINNER Reece from Essex.

THE WENGER ERA QUIZ

How much do you remember about the Arsène Wenger era? Here are 22 questions on his 22-year reign...

1. In which month and year did Arsène become Arsenal manager?

2. In which country was he managing immediately before becoming Arsenal boss?

3. Who made most appearances for Arsenal during the Wenger reign?

4. At which stadium did he manage his last Arsenal game?

5. Who was the youngest player to be given his debut under Arsène?

6. And who was the oldest?

7. How many FA Cups did Arsène win?

8. Which team did he face most often?

9. Who scored the first two goals of the Wenger reign?

10. Who was his last signing?

11. Name this player who Arsène signed from Monaco in 1997.

12. In which season did Arsène win his first double?

13. How many League Cup finals did Arsenal reach under Wenger?

14. What was Arsenal's biggest win under Wenger?

15. Fill in the missing word in this Wenger quote "In England you eat too much sugar and meat and not enough _____".

16. What was his overall win percentage? 52% or 58%?

17. How many times was Arsène named Premier League Manager of the Month?

18. Arsène offered to replay an FA Cup match because Arsenal scored a goal after not returning the ball to the opposition. True or false?

19. Who was Arsène's assistant manager between 1996 and 2012?

20. Who was the last player to make his debut under Wenger?

21. Which season is this picture from?

22. How many Arsenal games did he take charge of? 1,035, 1,135 or 1,235?

Answers on p61.

GUESS WHO?

There's been a bit of a mix-up with the latest Arsenal photoshoot. See if you can help us sort things out and identify these Arsenal headshots.

A	D	G
B	E	H
C	F	I

WORD FRENZY

Yet another mix-up! See if you can sort out the confusion and decipher these players' names.

1. Bill recent hero
2. Sulky intolerance
3. This reptile enchants
4. Hold mean enemy
5. Badly new neck
6. A saner mayor
7. Trash famous kind
8. Insanely still idea man
9. Social and sake
10 Link jeans corn

Answers on p61.

JOIN AS A JUNIOR GUNNER

Junior Gunners is the youth membership scheme for fans aged 0-16 years.
Our JG Members receive access to a range of exclusive benefits, including:

- Discounted match tickets.
- Opportunities to go behind the scenes, and meet Arsenal first-team players!
- Access to free family events.
- Weekly competitions, with prizes such as signed items and match tickets.
- The chance to be a mascot and part of the Arsenal Ball Squad.
- Access to the Junior Gunners app.
- An exclusive Membership Pack*.

*Full membership only.

There are three tiers of JG Membership;

- Welcome to our World 0-3,
- Team JGs 4-11
- Young Guns 12-16.

Each tier has access to its own targeted events and exclusive competitions.
To find out more and to join, head to www.arsenal.com/membership/junior.

QUIZ ANSWERS

PAGE 26 SPOT THE DIFFERENCE

PAGE 27 FOR THE RECORD

1. Nottingham Forest
2. 13
3. True
4. Score
5. 6-6
6. Ted Drake
7. Score as a substitute
8. Ian Wright
9. Cesc Fabregas
10. 722
11. Five
12. 2005/06
13. Arsenal's oldest Premier League player
14. Sparta Prague
15. Premier League assists

PAGE 55 WORDSEARCH

```
L  E  U  O  B  E  K  C  E  B  L  E  W
W  Z  J  A  R  T  E  T  A  O  N  O  B
T  A  M  P  T  K  T  N  D  A  L  T  L
H  N  U  T  Z  G  I  R  S  M  A  R  R
S  Q  Q  B  R  V  A  R  C  P  C  E  O
K  A  K  P  A  U  I  A  N  B  A  B  Y
V  R  G  H  D  M  Z  Q  Y  E  Z  L  A
Z  L  S  E  E  O  E  Z  M  N  E  I  B
W  R  N  J  R  N  G  Y  T  D  T  G  E
A  T  N  L  B  B  R  M  A  T  T  K  D
Y  J  A  J  H  K  A  Y  K  N  E  Q  A
N  P  T  T  G  C  C  F  C  E  G  F  X
K  G  I  R  O  U  D  T  K  R  V  T  D
```

PAGE 58 THE WENGER ERA QUIZ

1. October 1996
2. Japan
3. Patrick Vieira (402)
4. Huddersfield's John Smith's Stadium
5. Cesc Fabregas
6. Jens Lehmann
7. Seven
8. Chelsea
9. Ian Wright
10. Pierre-Emerick Aubameyang
11. Emmanuel Petit
12. 1997/98
13. Three
14. 7-0
15. Vegetables
16. 58%
17. 15
18. True
19. Pat Rice
20. Konstantinos Mavropanos
21. 2003/04
22. 1,235

PAGE 59 GUESS WHO?

A: Aaron Ramsey
B: Emile Smith Rowe
C: Hector Bellerin
D: Alex Lacazette
E: Eddie Nketiah
F: Reiss Nelson
G: Mesut Ozil
H: Mohamed Elneny
I: Shkodran Mustafi

PAGE 59 WORD FRENZY

1. Hector Bellerin
2. Laurent Koscielny
3. Stephan Lichtsteiner
4. Mohamed Elneny
5. Danny Welbeck
6. Aaron Ramsey
7. Shkodran Mustafi
8. Ainsley Maitland-Niles
9. Sead Kolasinac
10. Carl Jenkinson